You Are Here

Contemplations
for the Art of the Moment

TOM GEYER

Table of Contents

Preface *(Story)*

When I was a child, I participated in a makeshift international exchange facilitated by my next-door neighbor, who happened to be a French/American dual citizen. Her name was Madeline, and she was determined that I (at the age of fourteen) be exposed to French living. She would tell me that I would never become a proper man until I spent time in France—living as the French. La joie de vivre!

At that point in my life, I was showing evidence of never evolving out of being "momma's boy." I loathed the idea of being away from her and the comforts of home she had made for our family. I was so attached to my mother that I had separation anxiety when going to school. To imagine traveling across the Atlantic and living with a family I did not know was terrifying. But dear Madeline was a force to be reckoned with. She made it happen, and it happened quickly. That summer I was off on my first international flight to meet this odd family in Paris. Everything was uncomfortable.

Upon arriving, the only person in the family who spoke English was the boy (my age), named Didier. Didier could not have been more of an opposite. He was a French nationalist who seemed to only enjoy studying the history of France and sharing how it was the superior country: food, culture, etiquette, and military prowess. I, in contrast, wanted to skateboard, listen to music, and draw. That night, as I went to bed in an apartment only a few blocks away from the Arc de Triomphe, I found myself in a panicked state of dreadfully missing home. Yet somehow, I managed to get a few hours of sleep.

The next morning, Didier asked me if I wanted to go to the mall. I agreed as I had a goal of acquiring a pair of Guess jeans and some Vuarnet sunglasses. When we arrived, Didier mentioned he needed to go to the bookstore. I did not realize this meant he was going there to read an entire book (so he did not have to purchase it). At that point, I took a trepid yet daring step and said I would go shopping on my own. I left the one person I barely knew in an entirely unfamiliar city and ventured out on my own. The first thing I did was go to the map in the middle of the mall to find the stores that would interest me. This is when I had an awakening moment.

There on the map was a diagram of all the stores in the mall. Sitting in the middle of that map was a small red dot with words below that read: "Vous Etes Ici," You are here.

I am here.

Those three simple words washed over me like a rainfall. That moment, I saw the entire world extend from the map. I felt the stars beyond. I saw my mother and father in the United States doing their daily routine. All this was happening at the exact same time as I stood there in front of an illuminated map that read: "You are here." My presence and interconnection were unexplainable. I felt freedom to move about the world with the comfort of knowing that I am here with every step.

We live in only one place in this world, and it is here in the moment. What an amazing place, this moment. Here. Now. The only place you ever are.

When discovering this place (this awareness) you have a continuous opportunity. To remain. To observe. To receive. To do your art and nothing more. The art of the moment. You are already life, as is everyone and everything else. So, what is your art?

How we think, behave, and simply exist is the art. We are all connected to a higher energy that can serve us incredible peace and joy. It is our individual and collective responsibility to understand the world on this level so we can participate in harmony and prosperity for all. I refer to this connection as "enlightenment."

Our teachers surround us, and the events of the moment offer the practice ground to elevate our art. When we think, act, and exist in harmony with the moment, we feel it. When we think, act, and exist in disharmony with the moment, we feel it too. Everything we need to know is already here, now in the moment. Is it not our responsibility to be present and become masters of our art?

Introduction

Hello. Is there a common truth to life? I have recently returned to a point in my life where I asked this question in the midst of momentous loss and chaos. I was feeling a stout urge to reinforce my grounding with the insight and wisdom of past and current philosophers, prophets, and thought leaders. I deeply wanted to understand what common beliefs exist between the likes of Buddha, Lao Tzu, Jesus, Muhammad, Marcus Aurelius, Plato, Socrates, Mary Baker Eddy, Thich Nhat Hanh, Sadhguru, Dalai Lama, Eckhart Tolle, and Deepak Chopra—to name a few. Is there a theme to the big puzzle that may be staring us straight in the face? As so many have done, we may ask such a question in troubled times to understand why we are here and what purpose we serve.

Could we be missing something that would allow us to wake in the morning and know with certainty that what we set out to do has meaningful purpose? Or is this all just a crazy journey of unique experiences that turn out to be just another story that is quickly forgotten shortly after our bodies return to the soil? For what it is worth, allow me to share a glimpse into my crazy journey.

Succinctly, I am the son of a Unitarian engineer (my father) and a Christian Science artist (my mother). I will also add that another significant influence in my life came from my training as a martial artist where my sensei was an unusual Jewish lawyer. As I grew up, I started to question what I believed and the method I would use to center myself in belief.

Right from the start, a lesson I quickly understood was how diversity of thought, learning, and practice was a critical aspect of quality in life. I grew up never feeling as though I fit within a prepackaged mold. In fact, it was not until graduate school that I realized how most of my life was living through an "exception to the rule."

The very first day of graduate school we were asked to go around the room (about thirty students) and answer the following question: "What is something that is unique about you that you think would allow your class to remember you?"

When it was my turn to answer that question, I was inspired to say "I'm a twenty-three-year-old, middle-class, white, English-speaking male, who has been a minority most of my life." I said this without much thinking. Rather, it was simply a reaction as I found myself (at the moment) in a foreign school from another country talking to a group of students who came from all parts of the world. It reminded me that we were a group of disparate people from different pasts, religions, cultures, ethnicities, wealth, and so on, together in this room at the same time with a common purpose. I had spent my life among this abstract crowd—yet I have had the privilege of always being the token majority.

I was poor compared to my elementary school classmates. I was one of a few white people growing up in public schools of Baltimore. I was one of a handful of men in my college (which had just turned coed). And now here I am at a university in Belgium as one of only three Americans. I had also spent most of my childhood in a religion that did not believe in doctors helping you when you were sick or injured—and I had my fair share of serious illness and injury. Growing up, as many of my friends looked at me with both opinions and questions, I too, did the same.

I was inspired to share this with my newfound colleagues because this had become a comfortable place for me. I had gotten used to it, and with every step, I found such appreciation for vulnerability, unique perspectives, and common truths. The graduate program we were about to embark upon was a Master's Degree in Intercultural Management and Education (MIME). It felt like an appropriate context in that moment to say "hello" in a memorable way.

It is with this very same spirit that I am writing to you, with the following intention to diversely say "hello" in this moment.

Intention

The intention of this book is to be a slipway for self-exploration. It offers a common truth through varied perspectives and diverse starting points to explore your own practice of mastering the moment. Its intention is to experience each contemplation (pro re nata) as an arrangement for meditation, or simply to suggest a seed of an idea to plant in your consciousness and nurture while you live your life.

This book is not a "how-to" manual that answers or prescribes techniques to master the moment nor achieve high levels of enlightenment. That is up to you as we all have our own pathway to craft. Rather this book simply asks questions to consider as life offers its challenges that allow us to grow, overcome, and thrive.

With that said, let me open the book with one consideration I have found most decisively aids the discovery of a higher self. This one concept seems to be something that surfaces over and again in society.

Only when you let go of everything, do you discover I.

There is nothing more comforting, peaceful, joyful, and satisfying in this world of togetherness. Simply let go, and you will see what "I" means.

Common Truth

The predicating theory behind this writing is to suggest that many of the great thinkers and philosophers have been saying something very similar in history, that there is a common truth which surfaces as you consider the thinking, writing, and lessons of these prophets. What I realized, however, in the process of making this argument, is that it is not just these people. It is life in general. When it is realized, you see it everywhere.

Much like the coincidences when you lose a deep relationship and every song that comes on the radio seems to be about that loss. Every movie reminds you of the moments had. Each happening reminds you of how it was. It is peculiar how the message is present everywhere you look.

In this case, all of a sudden, there are signs that point to the fact that life is about surrender—letting go. Life is about releasing any issue and accepting that we are moving along our paths that lead to a higher understanding of ourselves.

It is a basic principle that when we let go of what we can, we experience a lightness (weight being lifted from our backs) that over time allows us to know who we are. As we do this, we are better able to understand the same plight that others are going through. The more we see that in both ourselves and those around us, the more compassionate we are able to be. We become kin to this moment: the here and now. As we experience this relationship with one another, we are able to understand our commonality (without judgment) in this continuous cycle of happenings that ultimately creates "life."

Common Truth Principles

1. Letting go uncovers enlightenment.
2. Letting go of everything allows you to discover yourself and therefore see others for who they truly are.
3. Being here in the moment allows us to participate in collective harmony with what is.

Contemplations

➊ Returning to "I"

Discovering oneself through the process of letting go is the foundation to the common truth. In so many of the works of philosophers in any part of the world and during any time, the concept of surrender resides. Letting go of what is most important for the betterment of life repeats itself continually in the history of humankind. Call it what you will: sacrifice, lent, atonement, celibacy, repentance, crucifixion, diet, it does not matter. Humans have continually looked to the idea of surrender for beneficial gain. Perhaps we are searching for a path to sanctity of truth.

One of the most predominant obstacles to this moment is found in each of us. It is our *ego.*

I propose:

Ego is a child who is forced to take the seat of "I" when you are preoccupied with events other than what is happening in the moment.

This child who is forced to take over observing the world on your behalf does so with limited wisdom and great fear. In fact, the lens by which the ego observes is limited in capacity to primarily search for what may seek to destroy it. Much like a child who sees monsters in the closet, behind the door, and under the bed, what the child sees is imagined and made real because of his or her fear. In some cases, the "predator" could appear to be you. Because of this, the ego may even try to convince you that it is better in the seat of observation and consciousness. The ego wants to prepare for, strategize, and, at times, assault its own deep-seeded fear and sense of insufficiency. We experience this happening through efforts of control, greed, resistance, defensiveness, avoidance, and aggression. Some of its strategies are quite clever, yet they never are successful at solving these fears because the ego, itself, is the obstacle. It stands upon the foundation of FEAR (False Evidence Appearing Real). When you reconnect with being (taking your seat of observing in the moment) and are no longer allowing the ego to be in charge, you cease to create these moments of tension, anxiety, worry, and grief.

What if ego is the source of suffering? Without it, might there be no pain? Could suffering be an illusion? Does not the pain from suffering happen when you are away from the moment? Many Eastern philosophies teach us suffering lives either in the past or the future. We, however, never live in either realm. It is impossible.

How many people are proud of their story as they regale within "the good times"? History. His story. Oftentimes, it becomes the story of identity. We have our whole notion of "self" invested in it. And, oftentimes, is not what we fear most the end to our story? As long as our ego is in control, what we fear most is our own moment of waking up. When we accept what is and let it pass without judgment, it becomes the death to our stress, tension, or drama in life.

Could it be possible: pain and suffering are evidence of ego's control? If ego were not in control, might there be less strife? Would there be suffering? Should ego be withdrawn, might we experience life absent of most fear?

Perhaps we also explore the intention behind ego. The intention of ego is clad in goodness. At the heart, it is not our enemy. It wants to protect you. Yet, does it not demonstrate over and again that its valiant efforts rarely flourish? We, the conscious guardians of the moment, should do with the ego as we do with children who are learning to become adults. Perhaps it is our responsibility to build a trusting relationship. What if we learned to lovingly discipline the ego and assure it that we will care for its survival, growth, belonging, and self-actualization in order for it to return to its protective house of our soul. Return home.

If you ever feel negativity in your life, can you take a pause and find stillness? Then, perhaps say to your ego (quietly or out loud): "I've got you. I've got your back." This process is one of the most basic ways to acknowledge that you are returning to the seat of consciousness (the "I") and putting the ego/mind back to a safe place of harmony.

❷ There Is a Gift in This Moment

Discovering Your Truth within the Present

Why do we look for anything other than what we have in the present? Here in this moment. Could what is "there" be irrelevant? Consider the value of all that is "here" now. If you believe what you are seeking is "there," some other place or time, perhaps you are stealing from yourself. Could you be depriving yourself of your birthright? Your body will tell you with its tension. If you are feeling unrest, try forgiving yourself for not being here. In the moment, when you completely accept your unrest/tension (no matter how small or large), might your struggles start to become calm? The opportunity is not out there. The opportunity is here—to let go of "out there" and receive what is right here in the moment. There is a phenomenon in the process of letting go of everything that is not here.

When life serves up difficulty, see this very moment as a perennial practice ground to avoid abandoning the gift of "here and now." Is it not interesting how we are automated to react to an occurrence and then lose sight of the next moment? It is like the experience, no matter how significant or trivial, somehow causes our mind to take over and reflect, contemplate, strategize, react, and lose sight of the miracle that follows. Jesus says: "Turn the other cheek." So true! The process of release or simply not grasping can be most transformative.

Be here and release your resistance

A master was walking with his student in the forest. The master pointed to a log lying askew and asked, "How much does that log weigh?" The student immediately saw this as a lesson in wisdom. He thought, how do I know the weight without picking up the log and feeling its heaviness?

After some time, he realized, "the only way to know best is to actually pick it up." Lifting the log, he told the master, "I believe it weighs fifty pounds." The master then said, "It weighs nothing if you aren't holding on."

Letting go of all that you carry and not picking up what is not yours can be an incredible path to nonresistance. There is nothing easier to do. Release. If your ego tries to trick you to believe that it is yours to carry, it is only doing so because it is frightened. Then, why not say, "I've got you dear friend; you are safe with me"? If we remain in the presence of the moment, perhaps ego will relax and let go too.

Let go to no longer fall. Let go to rise.

What is it that we pick up and carry along our life? How many labels do we identify with? Are they the truth of who we are? How many problems do we claim? Are they rightfully ours to carry? Might many or most of these labels and problems be false identity or false responsibility? Are you able to let them go and still be okay? As you let go of misappropriated obligation and false labels, how does it make you feel? Might you become lighter? Could it be the larger the label or task you let go of, the greater your lightness? Are you able to let go of some things? What about one more thing? Can you keep going? As you do, would you notice a new energy source opening? As the moment evolves, might the label disappear or the problem be solved on its own? As you let go of everything, might you discover that only one remains? Perhaps this one "gift" is rightfully yours as it is you in the moment. This oneness that remains is your sacred and unique truth. It is the seat of your consciousness that allows you to master your art within the moment of here and forever now.

Welcome.

❸ Identity to Revelation

How Do We Identify Ourselves?

Are we paying close enough attention to how we associate ourselves to (and within) this world? Not being whole or not feeling worthy or good enough may creep in to stake its claim. Deep desire, hope, or worry may justify its sensation. Could these thoughts and sensations of one's ego be searching for "evidence" of labels to identify with? Power, success, recognition, wealth, or perhaps that "someone" to complete you. Even when we obtain such things, might we realize that we are still not whole?

Where do we (and society) pay homage to success? Are they leading indicators to joy? Peace? Look at those who you think have made it to the top. Since the ego clings to labels, it needs to identify with external things: status, one's career, education, appearance, relationships, personal legacy, political affiliation, religion, sect/class, or other societal labels. Are these categories accurate representations of you? Are they accurate representations of others?

Have we ever felt good about imposed classifications? In this moment, how does it feel? What sensations are you experiencing as you contemplate this? Are you able to write down both the self-accepted identities and associated feelings? Perhaps spend some time with this list.

All of those things (that are not you) should be released at some point. Why not let go in this moment to discover your truth? As we have heard from so many philosophers, this is the process of "dying before death." If successful, you will realize that there is no end in death. Just as there is eternity in birth. This is the rhythm of life.

This is the core. It is the foundation of consciousness—the I. As we adjust to its purity, we might see a pure and simple world as well. Can you take back the "I"—the simple and true you? As you do, observe as you naturally reclaim the moment. Now you can allow the mind to be as it is, a device (fueled by the ego) that is used to solve trivial problems on the surface of life's events. It is a tool in the shed that can be pulled out when the proverbial grass needs cutting or hedges need pruning.

The mind is just a tool. However, when we seek ourselves in our thoughts and mistaken them for who we are, does it not then become our obstacle? We experience the obstacle when we are identifying with our past and imagining the status of our future.

Reflecting on the past or thinking about the future is not necessarily a bad thing. What determines "good" or "bad" is how present you are as you reflect or think. The chances are that you have to do very little reflecting or planning when you are here and now. Try not to use "thinking" as an excuse for why you should not be present. Presence taps into a wisdom that removes obstacles. Ruminating or strategizing for too long tends to obfuscate the power of presence.

Has life turned out as you planned? If so, perhaps we beg the question: "What is the purpose of life?" That is the only time we may want to propose that question. Otherwise, why not just do our very best to master letting life happen? You will do it in your own unique way. That is your art. It comes to you. You do not search for it. All you have to do is reveal your truth. Revel in its energy. Revelation.

❹ What You Seek Cannot Be Sought

Why the Outside Does Not Have the Answers

Consider this: All that you seek are idols that cannot give of themselves. In fact, they can become the hindrance to what you are searching for. Symbols tempt the mind rather than serve the spirit. We often search for a sense of guidance, identity, solidity, and fulfillment. Is this not a recipe for sensation and suffering? Nothing out there will satisfy you. People, things, and conditions might give you pleasure, but do they really grant you joy? Nothing external to you creates your joy. Joy cannot be taken. Nor can joy be taken away. It arises from within through one's peace of being. It is an essential part of the inner state of peace. The peace of the moment. It is your natural state of fully letting go of all things. Then is when you only have you. Then is when you are your truth. You have returned to the "uncarved block" that Taoism illustrates with such simplicity.

In martial arts, we have a story for earning different belts (representing maturity in the art). Everyone starts with a white belt. As we learn the art of combat, we darken our belt through our sweat, dirt from the dojo mat, and blood from our bodies. As we continue along our journey, we reach the moment of our belt becoming black. Full of experience. Full of martial skill. You have achieved what you have sought. Yet what you thought you were seeking became just the passageway to the art. That is then the new beginning. It becomes the gateway to a new journey—one of spirit. As you continue down this new journey, the blackness of the belt begins to fade and return to white. Darkness becomes the gateway to enlightenment.

"What is meant for you will reach you, even if it is beneath two mountains. What isn't meant for you won't reach you, even if it is between your two lips."

—Islamic Proverb

Seek nothing, not even your purpose. Instead prepare yourself to receive what is rightfully yours. This includes your purpose. There is no "take" in the world that is yours. Instead, all that is rightfully yours will come to you as you are ready. What are you doing to receive? Life is not yours for the taking. Rather, life is for the receiving.

Thy Kingdom Comes

Are you seizing the moment or are you preparing to receive it? When you receive what is rightfully yours, try just as quickly to let it go—that which is you will remain.

5 Centered in Stillness

Answers Are Found in Silence

Is life really getting busier and faster as we carry along? Could the progressive perception of speed and complexity in life be a result of the way we carry along? What if we stopped carrying? What if we no longer moved along?

Might it be that simple: just to remain still (while holding no weight in judgment)? Could this be where we discover calm, peace, and solution? Could it be that what we think in judgment causes the hectic perceptions and drama of our days? What if we were able to take a moment to just be still and observe? What might happen if we accept all that is as it is—without verdict? What if we let go of the desire to change what is happening around us by simply not judging the rightfulness or wrongfulness of the moment? Could we simply be centered in a stillness and silence to receive this moment without inspection? Could we replace the temptation for scrutiny with gratitude for the lessons within the moment?

What if we just remained still with it until that sense of "it" faded away or simply stopped being relevant?

If you consider all that has happened in your life, what "it" or "thing" has endured? Has there ever been something (a condition, situation, or perspective) that has always remained the same? Unchanged? Perhaps everything that changes has a guarantee to pass. However, should the answer to this question result in a "yes," then I ask if you might consider that which does not change to be your truth.

Oftentimes we are too impatient to simply let judgments or labels pass. What if we let the "it"—weight, label, fear, or worry—present itself as our teacher? All that has birth, life, and death comes and goes as the unchanging remains in a sanctity of stillness and natural order.

⓺ Be Your Own Teacher

How Do We Learn from Ourselves?

Because all necessary lessons exist here in the moment, it is important to open your eyes to many of the lessons that simply reside within your own body. Look no further than the process of how we nourish ourselves. We eat. We digest. We expel.

Perhaps we should see our own body as a vase with no bottom. Well . . . we have a bottom, but there is a hole there that allows us to let go of what is not ours. As we eat our food, we break it down through a process of chewing, swallowing, digesting, and excretion. The broken parts of the food send nutrients to all parts of our body (to maintain energy, prevent disease, heal illnesses, grow, and prosper). These parts of the food become the body. The rest is let go. Anything that is not released and does not immediately serve the body, can be stored but we all know what happens when we store too much. That hording process creates its own problems.

Just as the words you are reading in this moment, let the ideas stir in your mouth as you break them down and digest. Let the meaningful energy become a part of you. Then, let the remainder go. What is not used is unimportant in this moment.

Our body is not only the vessel that houses our being. It is the living, breathing blueprint for our own enlightenment. It houses all the "secrets" to experience a life of peace and joy. Perhaps all that you need for an enlightened life is nowhere else other than within your being. Have you not been born into this world with that right? You have all that you ever need within the depth of your clear understanding of you.

You, that center, have access to unlimited knowledge, vision, and wisdom in the moment. Now.

Listen, when you say: I know now. I see now. I understand now.

⑦ The Vase with No Bottom

Remaining Present in the Moment

"The sun illuminates only the eye of the man, but shines into the eye and the heart of the child. The lover of nature is he whose inward and outward sense are still truly adjusted to each other; who has retained the spirit of infancy even into the era of manhood."

—Ralph Waldo Emerson

Take note of innocence as it safeguards harmony. Is not innocence the ability to be free of wrongdoing—to be without harm to yourself or others? With innocence, there are no "sticking points" for resistance to cling.

Have you watched children scuffle at play? Should resistance ensue, they naturally search for a solution to reestablish harmony. It is not until the least flexible one snaps (lashes out, cries, or leaves) that we see the others move along to reestablish a more pleasant situation elsewhere. Usually, once that child has had time to calm down (letting go of the issue at hand) he or she will reconnect with the group and continue as if nothing had happened.

Maintaining or regaining presence in the here and now is the process for enlightenment—a return to innocence. You do this through the act of letting go of the past and not picking up issues in the present. Much like the monk in the forest, you carry no weight. If you cannot drop the sensation, then just accept the feeling of its energy and focus on the art of "stillness and patience." Are you able to sit with it until it falls off? The more you practice, the easier it becomes.

Continual presence of consciousness is unusual in today's world where ego takes the seat of observation far too often. In the meantime, when you sense negativity, might you be able to use it to your advantage? Here again is your training ground. When you feel "off," resistant, or if you sense discomfort, before going any further, take a pause and sit with the knowledge that you have picked it up. Be still with that moment. As soon as you do, you are in effect putting ego back in its place and taking the seat of consciousness where you belong. You are, once again, being present. This is your moment to master your art of letting go.

You are the vase to life that has no bottom. All the water, flowers, and greenery are entering that vase, which displays it well for just the moment. Can you be the observer who passes no judgment? Can you let go of needing to contain it? This act of surrender connects you to being. It takes you into the dynamic moment through nonresistance. Perhaps the best way to practice is by finding the little things of which to let go. Simply make note in a day or an hour. The important thing is to find them and set them free. Perhaps before bed, take inventory of those issues, concerns, or events that you have picked up in the day and set them free. Imagine a lake, where there is a raft that you can set these items upon and let go as a ceremonial pyre. Let them respectfully die as they drift away.

On a material level, it is the quality of your awareness in the present that will determine the eminence of your past and the predictive quality of your future. The art is your method of accepting all death as you accept all birth.

Not my will but thine be done.

8 Extremities of the Moment

What Is Our Role in the Extremes of Life

"Luck is as dangerous as misfortune. Hope is as hollow as fear. When you travel the ladder of judgement you find your position shaky. When you stand at the base with your feet planted firm, you will always keep your center."

—Lao Tzu

Lao Tzu proposes that life's experiences can be extreme. It is the concept of yin and yang. Danger creates safety. Loss creates birth. Disdain gives life to gratitude. Just as the blind man uses his stick to test the boundaries of the extreme, does he not wisely choose the way of the center?

There are extremes in life's journey. Why is our focus not maintaining our center? The ego will want to grasp the swinging stick and move off the center to the extreme. Its temptation is great. The more we can reside in the center, the less we need to partake in the extreme sensation of the outer edges.

Trauma and Misery

There are numerous accounts where someone has experienced trauma, by somebody or by perhaps a situation not even related to another human. These happenings can be significant where someone was wrongfully harmed in unthinkable ways that will forever change the manner that individual is able to exist. Many, including ourselves, will refer to this as being "victimized."

Can we address these experiences with the same consideration as in other contemplations? What happens in our life is not within our control (nor should it be). These are all experiences within the moment that challenge our ability to return to or remain in the moment and utilize the wisdom that comes from an enlightened state of being.

I put the quotation marks around "victimized" for a very specific reason. We are only victims when we allow our thoughts to label us that way. Do we not have the ability to shed ourselves of these labels just as we have accepted them? If you want a vivid sense of this, you can listen to the stories of countless war survivors, amputees, rape victims, children of domestic violence, the list carries on. Those who are able to overcome their life's situations all have one thing in common. They ceased to allow the label to be their identity. Many have taken different approaches to this outcome, but all have come to the same state of being. They have stood firmly in their truth. Oftentimes the severity of the experience has accentuated the firmness of their resolve.

If we are breathing, each of us has the exact same access to be centered in "I" and live within the realm of harmony. We have every ability to release all that is not ours and be at one with our essence, the great "I am."

We can find harmony most simply by being kind, to ourselves and to those around us. Does not kindness start with letting go of judgment? How hard do we need to be on ourselves? Others? The major oaks of Sherwood Forest are no greater and no less than the whistling thorn of the Serengeti. Each of us has our challenge to center ourselves in the moment of peace and joy. Letting go of judgment or comparison is an amazing technique in allowing that to happen.

Windfall and Euphoria

Just as sadness, worry, and suffering are manifestations or labels of the mind, so are elation and euphoria. These are simply sensations that exist at the other end of the spectrum. They too are just as treacherous and should be examined. One could say they are ego's imitation of joy.

The higher you rise, the harder you fall.

The intrinsic nature of euphoria can easily be confused with joy. The true telltale of differentiation is in the accompanying nature of stability and calm. When we are euphoric, excited, and elated, often we are not calm or stable. It is an extreme energy that is bursting of self-centric happiness. It is like winning the lottery.

I am on cloud nine! Cloud 9 is the king of the clouds. It is the highest level of cloud formation when compared to other clouds. A similar phrase we hear is being in "seventh heaven," which is the ultimate of heavens. It is the realm of heaven where God and her angels reside.

This self-centric happiness is easily noticed. Have you ever experienced someone who was this excited? It almost sucks all of the energy out of a room. Even if we selflessly love that person (without envy), we sense a selfishness in them that does not feel right. Oftentimes there is an inherent worry we have. We may say, "I hope this can sustain itself." We see this in scenarios such as instant love, quick wins, and unexpected windfalls. The stability and sense of calm does not appear to be in balance with the heightened level of energy. There appears to be an abandonment of wisdom. That is exactly what is happening. They are abandoning their consciousness at the presence of happiness as ego sits gleefully at the helm.

9 Learn from Your Natural Council

Nature Is a Master Teacher

At times, we may find life's situation offers incredible challenge. These circumstances can significantly bring out ego's greatest fears and worries—triggering the mind to take over through fear's logic. In these times, we may feel as though we have blinders on and cannot even begin to understand how to find our way back to our center. The pain, worry, and struggle are too great to find the "I."

In these cases, why not look no further than nature—our planet's council of teachers, masters of the art of the moment? Nature will always have the lesson to lessen the confusion of fear and see the light to your center. Not only are all the answers within you, but because of your connection to nature, they exist there too. The bird, the tree, the flower, the sun, the stars… are all teachers offering their wisdom day and night. Because all of nature only exists in this moment, they have no choice but to be in the present. They do everything in alignment with the way of life. When you look to nature for inspiration, why not do nothing but observe? Pay full attention without thought and with full appreciation that you and nature are kin. Then be still. Let nature do its work to offer you enlightenment. When it does, you will know. When you know, you might then say:

"*I now know.*"

The "I" will be your conscious presence. The "now" will be the moment. The "know" will be higher wisdom.

Nature is waiting for us to catch up. It waits so patiently doing its part to teach through its simple being (without words). It has the ability to teach through all senses: taste, touch, sight, sound, and smell.

Taste: Taste the presence of nature as you eat from it. Mindful eating is an incredible process to bring nature inside the body and experience its lesson of lessening. The simplicity of nature's taste can offer profound singular insight. Especially so, with the complexity of the foods we eat every day. As you experience this, try it with gratitude and abundant humility.

Touch: Let nature touch you: such as a cat that chooses to climb into your lap, lying down on a grassy field, or leaning up against a tree. Bathe or let your hand dip into a lake, your feet into an ocean. Let the physical connection to nature teach you the magnificence it has to offer through physical contact.

Sight: Pay undivided attention to nature. Watch a tree or flower as if you are seeing it for the very first time. Appreciate the work of art it represents. See the intelligence of its design. Pay attention to the function it provides to other animals. Observe with an empty and open mind.

Sound: Stand in nature and notice the cathedral it creates around you. Then, when you are able, close your eyes and experience that same cathedral without the information of sight. Listen to the message it has to tell. Hear it with full presence and no expectation. When you are listening, pay just as much attention to the silence as you do the sound. Oftentimes it is the silence that has more to say. That silence can also enhance the sound it concludes. When nature is quiet, there is a deep reason.

Smell: Walk through a garden on a summer's day, and smell the orchestra of aromas. Walk outside on a cold evening, and smell the crisp story of nature's activity. Take a walk in the morning, and smell nature's reaction to a new day. Nature's scent has a dynamic and responsive way to coordinate with light, wind, rain, and night. It plays a song to the soul through our nose that sings without words.

All of these approaches to learning from the profound wisdom and perfect design of nature will almost instantly inform you of your path to peaceful being. That nature is a reminder of your truth. You are connected with incredible cooperation.

Just as nature can be your teacher, our struggles can be destructive to that incredible source of guidance. Our resistance is a form of negativity as it is an internal battle with self, the ego. Negativity and resistance are synonyms for one another. Both are unnatural. Negativity can and will poison our bodies. Should we continue down a path of resistance or struggle, we are poisoning the earth as much as ourselves. It is okay. Nature will always prevail as it remains constantly present. However, when we find it tough to do it for ourselves, let us conjure extra strength to honor our teachers.

When the earth is ravaged and the animals are dying, a new tribe of people shall come unto the earth from many colors, classes, creeds, and who by their actions and deeds shall make the earth green again. They will be known as Warriors of the Rainbow.

—Hopi Prophecy

10 Part of the Whole, Whole of the Part

How Are We a Part of the Whole of Life?

"The Tao is always at ease. It overcomes without competing, answers without speaking, arrives without being summoned, accomplishes without a plan. Its net covers the whole universe. And though its mesh is wide, it doesn't let a thing slip through."

— Lao Tzu

How much more can we experience the intimacy of collective spirit, not just creating form, but being the countless facets of its own one nature—unity?

Observe our collective consciousness, those forever facets. Our perceptions are meant to be unique. This is the experience of love and compassion. Our own creative human life has no limits. Gaining, growing, and evolving perception. The transformation of creative change through perception. How much more is needed to realize this than through the nature of life itself? Can anything end the ongoing evolution? Do not all these facets ensure the guarantee? You—unique forever yet moving as they all do in the path of the Way.

It is not mysterious when even a cell of our own flesh is unique but also holds a secret code—a living, breathing blueprint of the entire body. In this moment, you are awake, alert, and clear about what Jesus said in his way: "I and the father are one."

I and the father, are one. The part and the all. The cell, the body, and the entire universe. The father, the daughter, and the Holy Spirit. Life will continue to unfold as it always has. The question we need to consider is "How aligned do we choose to be?" This will have immense effect in the harmony of progress and its progress of harmony.

"This thou must always bear in mind, what is the nature of the whole, and what is my nature, and how this is related to that, and what kind of a part it is of what kind of a whole, and that there is no one who hinders thee from always doing and saying the things which are according to the nature of which thou art a part."

—Thoughts of Marcus Aurelius (II-9)

11 Our Awakening on Earth

Our Collective Purpose

Could the world right now be an accurate reflection of the fearing, ego mind? Fear is an unavoidable consequence of ego's control. We live in a world of continuous birth and death, happenings and conclusions. Is it not an era of acceptance that we are challenged by? As a result, we find ourselves seeking a better situation: be it health, sanity, prosperity, freedom, or peace. Seeking is hanging on to what you have while trying to gain what you want. The moment we are able to let go of all that comes and goes, the sooner we are able to move to the next stage of our development. Can we see we are not separate from our own collective world?

Consider this: Should all insects cease to exist on this planet, it is estimated that all life on earth would end within fifty years. Even faster would be the planet's demise, should there be no worms. The same goes for our tress, plants, birds, and so on. However, should all humans no longer exist on earth, it would prosper.

We have shown a great ability to hurt this planet—as we take from its source to live beyond necessary means. And so far, we have not figured out our role in its prosperity. Perhaps we are its protector. Perhaps we will find a way to use our collective consciousness to not only preserve the ecosystem that works perfectly on its own but also be able to protect Earth from potential devastation outside of this planet.

Might how we see the world be how the world manifests itself? This is where the "light" can lead to the "dark." This is also where darkness can navigate to enlightenment. We all have our own worlds, but each one is a part of the whole. Revelation is what begins to align our worlds with unity and allows for a tipping point of mass awareness. Vision can iron out the insignificant wrinkles of life. With the precise vision, all else can fall into place. The macro overcomes the micro by the micro overcoming the macro. So when the majority of humans "move into the light" and become free of ego, might it not affect all of creation? Might we not observe a new world? Prophets of all corners of the planet have visions of this. Whether its Islam and "the Hour," Judaism and the Day of the Lord, Christianity and Judgment Day, Hinduism and Vishnu's return, there is a consensus of an awakening.

According to St. Paul, the whole of creation is waiting for humans to become enlightened: "*The created universe is waiting with eager expectation for God's sons to be revealed.*" John the Apostle wrote in Revelations: "*Then I saw a new heaven and a new earth. For the first heaven and the first earth had passed away.*" Lao Tzu gives reference to the universe patiently waiting for all creation of the three to master the two and allow the one to be free for all. In all cases, through our different and diverse perspectives, there is a common belief that a universal awakening is inevitable.

12 Death's Epiphany

What Can We Learn from Death?

Death mothers birth. The mother of death is birth. These are the threads of life's tapestry—having no opposite.

There is no greater a teacher than the experience of loss. Loss is what illuminates awakening, appreciation, and spiritual cleansing. The loss of a loved one, a cherished relationship, or a chapter of one's journey, through the experience of loss, we are able to see (perhaps over time) the sanctity and intrinsic value of that connection. Its purity is realized—as the unimportant and irrelevant details fade away or fall by the wayside. This moment is a precious baptism. It awakens us to the true nature of self. It is an atonement but not for any wrongdoing. Rather, it is an "at-one-ment." The cleansing unification of spirit.

We are all in this together. We are equals—all on our unique and coordinated journeys in a continuous life of death and birth. If we are able to let all be as we grow, we find enlightenment. If we are enlightened, are we not better able to be present for those we touch? When our needs for the external world are gone, might we notice that very same world improve greatly?

The Bird of Peace Takes Rest Upon Your Open Palm

Things that we thought we needed for happiness now can arrive with no struggle or effort. We are then free to enjoy and appreciate them while they last. Cycles will still come and go. But with each, there is no fear of loss. Life flows through our bottomless vase with ease. Even if things would collapse all around us, could we see it for what it is through the safety of deep inner peace? Might we feel the joy of life "joie de vivre" through this peace of mind?

13 Darkness: The Cleanser of Light

Darkness Is Our Gateway to Enlightenment

To understand the concept of darkness, may I suggest we first remove the stigma of the word? Darkness is simply the absence of light. It is a place that forces one's sight to close down. If we stand in a well-lit room, we are easily able to see its contents. There is that chair. I can see those books on the shelf. There is a candle in a candlestick holder sitting upon the wooden table. All is clear with light in this room. Identity is vivid.

When the light is then turned off, the identity of those items goes away. I can no longer even see the outline of my hand as I wave it in front of my face. All objects are still there in form and presence. The labels are gone. The energy remains. We find ourselves in the cave of darkness, the tomb of Christ. Here, we are forced to practice fearlessness. It becomes a place to overcome ego's control of one's life, an opportunity to regain creative control. Here, you are closer to a divine and consecrated moment. Can you find your ease without labels of judgment? The transformation of ego's mind to spiritual mind is taking place. Good and bad become one. The vastness of extreme become the wholeness of peace.

If it feels like a black hole, then is it not that, the nursery of the birth of stars themselves? If it feels like being in the womb of the holy mother, then is it not rich with all potential? If it feels like the darkest night, is the night not what lays the land to rest and breath, so it may be that growth of day for the plant, tree, bird, or animal? Is it not the opportunity for regeneration and rejuvenation?

Here, in darkness, is the ease to be aware of the true you and the world and universe around. The prejudices, the discriminations, the critiques . . . lessen, lessen, lesson . . . about the self, about the world around. Can you take this precious moment in the quiet now? Feel the profundity and purity of you. Here in this simple cave you are experiencing why the Buddha says "ignorance is illusion." Is not the illusion the label of ignorance? The part is the all and the all is the part. One knows his or her own life, and one is all life. Death ends in darkness, this sacred tomb. The continuity of your life is felt.

Darkness is therefore a friend, a teacher, or a rite of passage to greater understanding. Any event that leads to darkness (crisis, emergency, or circumstantial erosion) should be received with gratitude and honor.

Are you able to cooperate with it rather than fight or avoid it? Why not welcome it in without judgment? As the situation presents itself, experience and respect all of it. If it feels too strong and bumpy, go deep into your seat of consciousness. Be like the whale at the bottom of the ocean. Allow the waves to crash at a safe distance. It is simply energy with an incredible gift. Experiencing its truth presents a new vantage point and transforms any chaos in a loving and tender embrace of forgiveness and peace.

The same can apply for others. Should you see struggle in others, can you respond by holding their truth in that same deep peace? Do not react. Instead, take time to respond. Know that struggle cannot exist with presence. Wherever this person may be, your relationship to this person is here, now, allowing you to be aware and calm in its presence. It is offering this moment where all things and all beings are in alignment with this tapestry of life. Do nothing. Just be forgiving.

Whether it is with others or within yourself, if you forgive every moment, are you not allowing it to be as it is? *For-give*: the etymology of the word insinuates that you are in the complete moment and are giving it away. Through this practice, there is no resentment. This type of forgiveness is acceptance without judgment through love. It is the recognition of the irrelevance of the past through the loving continuity of the moment. It is a sacred and quiet place with intense presence within and all around you. It is through this realm of being that we then are able to for-"get."

14 Time: A Theory of Relativity

What Is the Real Value of Time?

We live in a world where time is considered one of the most scarce and valuable assets. The older we become, the more precious it seems to be. Perhaps we consider that time is not what is so valuable. Rather, time is simply relative. Perhaps the "gift" that is most inimitable is the only thing that is not found in time—the present moment. As our clock keeps turning, the present remains still.

The more we are focused on the future and past, the less we are able to be present—the most dear thing there is. This is where collective life unfolds. This is also the only point of access to this magnificent collective energy (connected to all other forces of the universe). Another way to look at this is through the statement "Time slows down (stops) when you are in the moment." Your consciousness has crossed over from time to presence. Some call this "the zone."

Nothing ever happens in the past. It is happening right now—right here. Nor will anything occur in the future. The question is, how conscious and alert are you while it is all happening? This awareness of the moment is what taps into incredible insight, energy, and creativity, allowing you to truly be in the zone. This deep connection to the present moment allows you to demonstrate your art in a way that is profound and unique to your truth.

The past is a memory. The future is a mystery—a prediction. Who are we to imagine what could be? What matters is our awareness of the present, right here and now. In life-threatening situations, you get a glimpse of this. Suddenly everything seems to slow down. You are dramatically being pulled into the moment. If you have been in an automobile accident, you might relate. When thinking about the experience, it was as if everything went into slow motion. You could see each millisecond of the experience.

As a martial artist, we experience this in combat. When we engage in battle, the world tends to slow down dramatically as the awareness of one's surrounding becomes greater. This is what we practice in its art. It is the art of being aware of and comfortable in this moment that you are able to perform your craft with grace and mercy. Those who engage in combat who do not have this wisdom will fall to the mercy of the master.

Another example of time slowing is found with boredom. Have you experienced how slowly time passes when you are bored? Boredom is idle existence within the moment. You are viscerally aware of the moment when you have nothing to do but to simply observe. Pay attention to its quiet stillness. Open yourself to receive the insight that is rightfully yours. Often, this is explained as the "small and quiet voice." It is not a voice you hear. Rather, it is a voice you feel. The next time you have this blessed opportunity ask "What at this moment is missing?" If you are truly present, you might say "nothing."

 Healing

Discovering Health in the Moment

With any physical pain or injury, is there not an automatic response your body commences called healing? Can you imagine what life would be like without healing? This world is filled with recovery, rejuvenation, restoration, and triumph. There is no difference with disease. *Dis-ease*. Lack of ease. We do the same work for all cases. We overcome.

The power of disease these days is that each type has been given a label, and that label (each one of them) has been marketed to become an ominous belief on a global basis. A consensus. Have these labels been defied and proven wrong on individual accounts? Yes. Each and every one of them.

Fear of extinction is human. Thankfully, so is resilience.

The above statement is a subtitle from *The Atlantic* news article written in June 2016. The headline read "Why Hasn't Disease Wiped out the Human Race?"

We are a resilient society of animals. We have survived every virus, disease, injury, and illness. Not to be cavalier, as this is a contentious subject relative to belief systems, but may I suggest we put our best foot forward in all approaches to healing and restorative health? No doctor, scientist, or religious authority would disagree that all human consciousness, attitudes, and behaviors, which desire and focus to dismantle the stigma of illness, is productive.

All labels are a "hook" for ego to grasp and claim its reason to sit in the seat of "I" and look after your very survival. This is again fear rearing its head and justifying the validity of and respect for the horror of death and decay.

Instead of identifying yourself to the label, let us let that go. The path to letting it go can happen however you choose. Having grown up in a Christian Science household, I have seen the path of overcoming illness without the assistance of anything more than prayer. However, why cannot our fellow colleagues, brothers, sisters, and nature do their part to contribute to dismantling the label of illness? The path is yours. The key to the gateway along this path, however, is knowing your truth.

Finding peace and calm amid any injury or illness is always helpful for healing. Allow it to do its work along whatever path you pursue. Finding peace and calm in the moment will inextricably harness the power of healing. There is no disease in the moment's presents.

16 **Finding Comfort in Uncertainty**

How Do We Find Peace in Unfamiliar Situations?

What If the Moment Causing Uncertainty Has Happened?

Have you ever had a moment come about where you did not understand why it happened? You spend unimaginable time trying to figure out what had happened and why it happened. What was the reason for it? Was it something I did? Is there a greater force out there against me?

Each one of these questions is ego energized. Might it be possible to give up trying to understand the cause and message? There is no importance in the cause nor the message. It already happened. It is passed. Where are you now? Are you here? Here in this moment? If so, you do not need answers. You have them. Here. Now. You simply have to pay attention.

If there is one aspect of life that provokes, antagonizes, and threatens the ego, it is the realm of uncertainty. Uncertainty stokes the flame of fear. The present is limitless with energy (positive or negative as it makes no difference).

The unconscious ego greatly fears this arena of exhausting anticipation that pulls the countless tensioned cords of one's past by the infinite possibilities of one's future and harnesses its focus of the never-ending question: "What now?"

What? Now?

Yes, dear ego. Now.

The moment of now is what brings back the conscious you: quietly, calmly, and openly accepting the infinite gifts of the present. Being here, you are alert, aware, empty, and a part of the immense and sacred whole. You are prepared with your spiritual wisdom to watch, learn, and do as little as necessary to leave nothing left undone.

Can you surrender this instant to the pure loving reality of the moment that stands here around you?

What If the Uncertainty Is Happening Now?

When you experience the moment of uncertainty taking shape, remaining firmly in the seat of this moment will allow you to be best prepared to handle the occurrence. As the event is unfolding, can you first be the still witness to the event? Might that simple effort benefit you greatly? Think of first responders and the way they are able to handle dramatic situations.

If you have had a loved one rushed into the emergency room, oftentimes the initial feeling is that the hospital workers are not responding with the level of urgency you might hope for. Some of that is due to your own fear and ego-mind speeding up time. Another part of that perspective is the responders being still and observing the moment as time slows down for them.

The front office, nurses, and doctors appear to be taking their time. Even in situations where the patient is severely injured, a doctor does not raise her energy level much, if at all. This is not because she does not care. Far from it. She is observing what is happening and taking methodical steps to ensure "triage" is completed without mistake and in the most expeditious fashion.

Emergency medical technicians, police, soldiers, firemen, and lifeguards are all taught to remain calm in urgent situations and observe what is happening before taking action. This process is proven to be highly effective at efficiently managing the uncertainty of crisis. It not only ensures that the exact situation is successfully being addressed, it also prevents the situation from becoming a further catastrophe.

This principle holds true in hostage negotiations, political debates, physical combat, and daily routines. "Taking a moment." Being here and now is what taps into a deep pool of wisdom that will forever provide an intelligence, intuition, and creativity that will have no uncertainty. It will know, guide, and lead you to an outcome beyond your immediate comprehension. Here, you will find incredible comfort.

It may sound strange, but you will find peace in chaos. Peace is what delivers comfort. It is also what allows you to remain calm and offer love in what appears to be the most tumultuous of times.

17 Helping and Teaching Others

Helping and Supporting Others

Being with Others

As we continue along our journey of the moment, we may experience others (friends, family, and strangers) who feel comfortable sharing their life's desires, complications, and frustrations. As you are more familiar being present, the reality of other humans should become clearer. Your relationships become visceral. You are able to see others' true being behind the facade of their body and mind. You may also see them without judgment (your own ego has let go). Behind that façade will be their beautiful truth. When confronted with someone's conditioning of sensation (their ego) and unconscious behavior (their façade), you remain present in the moment of love and compassion as you experience the other person's radiance and pure being. In this case, perhaps, all the presented conditioning is just an illusion—built upon fear. Is not compassion a deep bond and awareness of all creatures as perfect?

Helping Others

Helping others first requires that we understand how to help. If we see others already as perfect, how can we truly help them? The way to help others in need is to be present and simply practice compassion. Treat that other as an honored guest. Be welcoming, attentive, and gracious. Can you lose any distraction and honor that person's presence with your pure consciousness and attention? Are you able to see the person's truth rather than how he or she has been conditioned through his or her experiences in life? Is the other person not your equal, a perfect soul past his or her veil of conditioning and ego? Everyone has his or her own journey, and as another person presents himself or herself to you, is it not your honor to greet him or her as a weary traveler? Listen to what each person says so you can become aligned in spirit. Allow each person to shine as you listen to his or her story.

As your guest becomes eased, he or she may show you what is on the other side of the mask: the ego's deep worry, fear, anxiety, desire, and emptiness. Again, can you allow that gift to be given with loving presence as you see deeper into the radiant soul that stands before you? Be patient and let the gifts flow by as they arrive. All the while, see and appreciate each person's truth. It is significant to understand your help as being a mirror of another person's truth rather than an enabler of his or her ego or will. Much of your assistance requires very little action as this is their journey rather than yours.

Teaching Others

The highest form of teaching requires no words or actions. It simply comes from being. Teaching is no different than being present with nature. The first step is experienced in your own practice of being (not showing, speaking or problem solving). This "being you" allows other people to judge their level of interest, attraction, allure, and magnetic pull. That is the way.

Should they ask for opinion, guidance, and council, can you be still and respond with love, kindness, and question? We are often tempted to react to others with our own life experience in the form of rules, demands, and strategies. The problem with that approach is you may be denying this person the gift of owning the next step in his or her journey. In fact, with the right advice, you risk stealing the person's ownership of growth and success.

Instead, how might your wisdom and insight go one step further and offer your response with a question? This does two things. It allows you to listen deeper to the nuances of the person's dilemma while further being with his or her pure consciousness. It also allows the person to answer.

They then own the step. It will be experienced as their choice, declaration, and destiny.

Guidance is about principles rather than intelligence or actions. Intelligence is skill—easy to acquire. Action is tact—rules of engagement that change in the moment. But principles are wisdom, universal awareness that applies to all aspects of life's situation. Teach through being. Emanate pure consciousness. Move about the world with the comfort of knowing that you and those around you are here with every step. When considering this, should not our role as individuals be to live a life where we are aware and accepting of what is without judgment? Then is when we can eliminate suffering on the level of causation—by eliminating fear from the world. Much like our natural masters (the tree, the flower, and the animal), who you are is much more vital a method of teaching (and more powerful a purifier of the world) than what you say and more essential even than what you do.

If you have the answer, can you refrain from saying it? Can you take a moment to ask the best question? The one rule . . . no rules. In the moment, you will know what is right.

18 True Love

This concept is one that radiates immense energy. If I could suggest that we do not necessarily limit this to romantic love, however. It can be romantic. It can also be available to all aspects of the world and universe. Experiencing, receiving, and offering true love is the greatest form of compassion, empathy, and altruism. It is seeing another for who the person is with no selfish intention or desire. It is not even generosity nor is it personal sacrifice. Those who you truly love need nothing from you. They are perfect as they are. They need nothing because we know that everything they need is already located within their being.

I do not want to insinuate that we do not care for, protect, share with, contribute to, and champion others we love. This is far from the truth. The starting point of our interactions with those we truly love, however, comes from allowing them to shine on their own.

Consider an example of a mother or a father raising a child. We see their perfection as soon as birth arrives. Mother and father nurture the infant's needs but always with an intention of self-sufficiency. We will die for our children without any consideration. The unconditional nature of our relationship lasts for as long as we are able to see their truth and the unique value they bring to the world. We are their champion, friend, disciplinarian, advisor, counselor, and advocate. However, we offer this support patiently and quietly from the background with no desire for recognition. Their success invites joy into our lives. Their triumph sews a garden of inner peace. If parents let ego interfere, we see how our children respond with fear, anxiety, and turmoil. They train us as much as we train them. This is true of all beings. If we are wise to this, we find ways to align as each individual grows and supports one another to prosper.

The really cool thing about love is that it is endless, tireless, and joyful. What would happen if we truly loved all beings? True love. One that has no "take" in it. One that has no identity associated with it.

Can you love your child, mate, colleague, neighbor, neighborhood, city, state, nation, or world? Can you love your enemy? That is the only way to have no enemy.

II. Momentum through Practice

How Do We Master Our Art?

How many ventures have we made in life to accomplish something seemingly important? Yet, after some effort, we move along and never really allow it to stick? Why does this happen? Diets, exercise, hobbies, and so on. We tend to see it as extracurricular, kind of like a fix. I will do something to fix the problem and then return to my old way of doing things that got me here to start. Why?

If something bothers you to the point where you want to correct it, why not follow through? If something intrigues you because you see the benefit it would provide for your life, why not include it in your repertoire? Making a change that sticks requires that we turn a "fix" into a practice. Much like a doctor, engineer, lawyer, athlete, or any other skilled individual, we create a practice that becomes valuable in the world.

Having a practice is something we can relate to. It is a way of doing something as a lifelong behavior that improves over time. We simply need to see that behavior as a way of life. A new ingredient or the removal of an ingredient (one that perhaps is not working well) for the type of life we choose.

When we look at it this way, are we better able to figure out how to work this change into our daily routine and have it become a part of who we are? Might we then practice with a level of moderation and ease that is not typically done when we are trying to fix something? Then, over time, that practice of our practice can evolve into our art. When we reach the art, we find a new level of mastery through philosophy.

The Ease of Mastery

First, let us articulate the difference between "mastery" and perfection. To be a master, you do not need to be perfect. You need perfect intention, but to hold a daunting definition of perfection above your art is nonproductive as well as inaccurate. Mastery of your art is simply reaching a level where it is no longer about the skill. Rather it is about utilizing that skill in a way that goes beyond the skill itself. It transcends the basics (the what) and becomes an eloquent and alluring force with its own magnetic draw and intrigue (the why to the how). It is a transcendence from action and mechanics to a philosophy and a way.

"Don't practice until you get it right. Practice until you can't get it wrong."

—Misty Copeland

When people begin to master their art, they discover the philosophies that serve as their guiding force—their gift. Look no further than what others see in their incredible path and observe how they, too, establish mastery.

Muhamad Ali, Frank Lloyd Wright, Virginia Woolf, and Frida Kahlo: each of these masters made his or her art look so easy, effortless, and intriguing. Had you asked them, they would say it is easy. They truly loved what they did. They had mastered their skills through practice and philosophy—creating art. Within that art, came inspiration that was shared. The master of skill becomes the philosopher of life.

"Impossible is just a big word thrown around by small men who find it easier to live in the world they've been given than to explore the power they have to change it. Impossible is not a fact. It's an opinion. Impossible is not a declaration. It's a dare. Impossible is potential. Impossible is temporary. Impossible is nothing."

—Muhammad Ali

*"You can't make an architect. But you can open the doors
and windows toward the light as you see it."*

—Frank Lloyd Wright

*"If you do not tell the truth about yourself,
you cannot tell it about other people."*

—Virginia Woolf

*"Pain, pleasure and death are no more than a process for existence.
The revolutionary struggle in this process is a doorway open to intelligence."*

—Frida Kahlo

Conclusion: Here, You Are

Enjoy

"The way to get back to yourself is to literally get still and be alone and to drown out the voices of the world so that you can find your own way, because your own way is always right here.... You can spend all the years of your life looking outside of yourself for the answers to "why am I here?" and "what am I really supposed to do?" but only when you are conscious enough to connect to the stillness can you really find the answers."

—Oprah Winfrey

Remember that all you ever need is right here—right now. There is no journey required to distant places to discover purpose, joy, or peace. It is right here, rightfully yours.

Release and remain still. Stillness in thought, motion, and energy is what delivers your gift of knowledge that connects us all together for the benefit of ourselves. Through the perfect design of universal love, difference becomes similarity. Darkness sheds light. Fear becomes peace. Practice becomes principle. Perpetual death and birth contribute to the eternity of life. We are now free. We are free to move about the world with the comfort of knowing that we **are** here (as one) in this moment.

Afterward

Afterward

Quintessential Teachings

I would like to share what I have found to be examples that support the original consideration that "letting go to discover oneself as you see all others for their truth in this moment" is supported at critical times with other well-known prophets, philosophers, and thinkers. I have found the following examples as key documented points in time that support this argument. I have also included an array of quotes from notable people as a reference to the continual resurfacing of this thesis.

Siddhartha Buddha

Buddha's first teachings after enlightenment are known as the four noble truths. These truths are Dukkha (**suffering/sensation**), Samudaya (**origin of suffering/sensation: attachment**), Nirodha (**cessation of suffering/sensation: letting go of attachment**), and magga (**the eightfold path**). Following his sutra, with the full understanding of these four truths, a release from samsara (reincarnation) is achieved.

"Unprovoked is my release. This is the last birth. There is now no further becoming." It is through the fourth noble truth that the eightfold path is established.

Just this noble eightfold path: right view (**virtuous beliefs**), right aspiration (**non-sensuality**), right speech (**truth and kindness**), right action (**virtuous behavior**), right livelihood (**following your passion**), right effort (**establishing harmony**), right mindfulness (**awareness in the moment**), right concentration (**meditation and insight**). That is the ancient path, the ancient road, traveled by the Rightly Self-awakened Ones of former times. I followed that path. Following it, I came to direct knowledge of aging & death, direct knowledge of the origination of aging & death, direct knowledge of the cessation of aging & death, direct knowledge of the path leading to the cessation of aging & death. I followed that path. Following it, I came to direct knowledge of birth … becoming … clinging . . .craving … feeling … contact … the six sense media … name-&-form … consciousness, direct knowledge of the origination of consciousness, direct knowledge of the cessation of consciousness, direct knowledge of the path leading to the cessation of consciousness. I followed that path.

Marcus Aurelius

Aurelius frequently discusses the concept and value of being in the present throughout the collections of his manuscript *Meditations*. I have chosen just one of his entries to signify this core tenant of virtuous and meaningful living. I have chosen to highlight the sixteenth verse in his second book as it so aligns with the first teachings of Buddha.

The soul of man does violence to itself, first of all, when it becomes an abscess, and, as it were, a tumor (**attachment**) on the universe, so far as it can. For the vexed at anything which happens is a separation of ourselves from nature (**the here and now**), in some part of which the natures of all other things are contained (**letting go for harmony**). In the next place, the soul does violence to itself when it turns away from any man, or even moves towards him with the intention of injuring, such as are the souls of those who are angry (**virtuous mind and behavior**). In the third place, the soul does violence to itself when it is overpowered by pleasure or by pain (**sensation/suffering**). Fourthly, when it plays a part, and does or says anything insincerely and untruly (**truth**). Fifthly, when it allows any act of its own and any movement to be without an aim, and does anything thoughtlessly and without considering what it is, it being right that even the smallest things be done with reference to an end: and the end of rational animals is to follow the reason and the law of the most ancient city and polity (**mindfulness and kindness**).

Jesus

There is arguably no greater moment with Jesus's teaching than his Sermon on the Mount to symbolize his philosophy and wisdoms throughout the remainder of his life. The Sermon on the Mount is the longest discourse of Jesus's teachings found in the Bible. As well, the sermon was the first record of his teaching following his baptism and forty-day retreat (temptation of Christ) within the Judaean desert where he experienced his purpose. Upon returning he gathers his disciples and shares his ministry.

Here is where he describes the character of those in the kingdom of heaven as "blessed"

Blessed are:

- the poor in spirit: for theirs is the kingdom of heaven. – *letting go*

- they that mourn: for they shall be comforted. – *sensation*

- the meek: for they shall inherit the earth. – *present and still*

- they which do hunger and thirst after righteousness: for they shall be filled. – *virtue*

- the merciful: for they shall obtain mercy. – *kind*

- the pure in heart: for they shall see God. – *aligned through innocence*

- the peacemakers: for they shall be called the children of God. – *harmony*

- they which are persecuted for righteousness' sake: for theirs is the kingdom of heaven. – *virtuous behavior*

- ye, when men shall revile you, and persecute you, and shall say all manner of evil against you falsely, for my sake. – *fearlessness*

- Rejoice, and be exceeding glad: for great is your reward in heaven: for so persecuted they the prophets which were before you. – *find joy*

As well, it was here at his sermon that Jesus taught his disciples to let go of materialism and judgment and find goodness in God's kingdom. He concludes this through what is known as the Lord's prayer.

Our Father who art in heaven, hallowed be thy name. Thy kingdom comes. Thy will be done, in earth as it is in heaven. Give us this day our daily bread. And forgive us our debts, as we forgive our debtors. And lead us not into temptation, but deliver us from evil. For thine is the kingdom, and the power, and the glory, forever.

Mary Baker Eddy

After years of studying the Bible, Eddy wrote "the scientific statement of being" as a declaration that embodied the truth of existence. She believed this concept to represent the relationship that one has with God. She wrote this statement intentionally to be about the moment (now) and truth of human existence. This essence of Christian Science proposes that humankind should release "material-focused mind" and see their "spiritual existence" as truth.

There is no life, truth, intelligence, nor substance in matter. All is infinite Mind and its infinite manifestation, for God is All-in-all. Spirit is immortal Truth; matter is mortal error. Spirit is the real and eternal; matter is the unreal and temporal. Spirit is God, and man is His image and likeness. Therefore, man is not material; he is spiritual.

Common Quotes

Compassion

What you do not wish for yourself, do not do to others. – **Confucius**

Do unto others as you would have others do unto you. – **Jesus**

Humankind has not woven the web of life. We are but one thread within it. Whatever we do to the web, we do to ourselves. All things are bound together. All things connect.– **Chief Si'ahl (Seattle)**

Letting Go

Let reality be reality. Let things flow naturally forward
in whatever way they will.

– Lao Tzu

Letting go all else, cling to the following few truths.
Remember that man lives only in the present, in this fleeting instant:
all the rest of his life is either past and gone, or not yet revealed.
This mortal life is a little thing, lived in a little corner of the earth;
and little, too, is the longest fame to come - dependent as it is on
a succession of fast-perishing little men who have no knowledge
even of their own selves, much less of one long dead and gone.

– Marcus Aurelius

No one knows whether death, which people fear
to be the greatest evil, may not be the greatest good.

– Plato

"Some people believe holding on and hanging in there are signs
of great strength. However, there are times when it takes
much more strength to know when to let go and then do it."

– Ann Lander

Flow with whatever may happen, and let your mind be free:
Stay centered by accepting whatever you are doing. This is the ultimate.

– Zhuang Zhou

Sometimes you have to let go to see
if there was anything worth holding onto.

– Socrates

Seek not that the things which happen should happen as you wish;
but wish the things which happen to be as they are,
and you will have a tranquil flow of life.

– Epictetus

It is not the actions of others which trouble us
(for those actions are controlled by their governing part), but rather
it is our own judgments. Therefore, remove those judgments and resolve
to let go of your anger, and it will already be gone. How do you let go?
By realizing that such actions are not shameful to you.

– Marcus Aurelius

To fear death, my friends, is only to think ourselves wise,
without being wise: for it is to think that we know what we do not know.
For anything that men can tell, death may be the greatest good
that can happen to them: but they fear it as if they knew quite well that
it was the greatest of evils. And what is this but that shameful ignorance
of thinking that we know what we do not know?

– Socrates

A man is rich in proportion to the number of things
he can afford to let alone.

– Henry David Thoreau

Sometimes letting things go is an act of far greater power
than defending or hanging on.

– Eckhart Tolle

People have a hard time letting go of their suffering.
They prefer suffering that is familiar to the unknown.

– Thich Nhat Hanh

Let it all go, see what stays.

– Rajneesh (Osho)

There are two ways to be.
One is at war with reality and the other is at peace.

– Byron Katie

Life moves on and so should we.

– Spencer Johnson

The beautiful journey of today can only begin
when we learn to let go of yesterday.

– Steve Maraboli

To resist change, to try to cling to life, is like holding your breath:
if you persist you kill yourself.

– Alan Watts

The first half of life is devoted to forming a healthy ego,
the second half is going inward and letting go of it.

– Carl Jung

"The day I understood everything, was the day
I stopped trying to figure everything out.
The day I knew peace was the day I let everything go."

– C. JoyBell C.

I don't let go of my thoughts, I meet them with understanding,
then they let go of me.

– Byron Katie

In order to be what we are,
we have to come out of being what we are not.

– John Butler

Do not run away; let go.
Do not seek; for it will come when least expected.

– Bruce Lee

Being Here and Now

Observe things as they are and don't pay attention to other people.

– Huang Po

Sticking with the uncertainty, getting the knack of relaxing
in the midst of chaos, learning not to panic – this is the spiritual path.

– Pema Chödrön

The present is the only place you can be.
If you live, you live in this moment.
If you die, you die in this moment. This moment is eternity.
How are you going to escape it, even if you try?

– Sadhguru

Life gives you plenty of time to do whatever you want
to do if you stay in the present moment.

– Deepak Chopra

Let go of the battle. Breathe quietly and let it be. Let your body relax
and your heart soften. Open to whatever you experience without fighting.

– Jack Kornfield

There are only two days in the year that nothing can be done.
One is called "yesterday" and the other is called "tomorrow".
Today is the right day to love, believe, do and mostly live.

– Dalai Lama

It is said an Eastern monarch once charged his wise men to invent him a sentence to be ever in view, and which should be true and appropriate in all times and situations. They presented him the words, "And this too, shall pass away." How much it expresses! How chastening in the hour of pride! How consoling in the depths of affliction!

– Abraham Lincoln

The present is the same for everyone; its loss is the same for everyone: and it should be clear that a brief instant is all that is lost.
For you can't lose either the past or the future; how should you lose what you don't have?

– Marcus Aurelius

You don't always have to be doing something.
You can just be, and that's plenty.

– Alice Walker

"The Perfect Man uses his mind like a mirror - going after nothing, welcoming nothing, responding but not storing."

– Zhuang Zhou

When hungry, eat your rice; when tired close your eyes.
Fools may laugh at me, but wise men will know what I mean.

– Linji Yixuan

God gives you His spiritual ideas, and in turn,
they give you daily supplies. Never ask for tomorrow:
it is enough that divine Love is an ever-present help; and if you wait,
never doubting, you will have all you need every moment.

– Mary Baker Eddy

"You have only to rest in inaction and things will transform themselves. Smash your form and body, spit out hearing and eyesight, forget you are a thing among other things, and you may join in great unity with the deep and boundless."

– Zhuang Zhou

Feelings are just visitors. Let them come and go.

– Mooji